THE ANTOINETTE MATLINS "*RIGHT-WAY*" SERIES
ON USING GEM IDENTIFICATION TOOLS

DICHROSCOPES
Made Easy

The "RIGHT-WAY" Guide to Using Gem Identification Tools

D1462179

ANTOINETTE MATLINS, PG, FGA

GEMSTONE PRESS
Woodstock, Vermont

www.gemstonepress.com

Dichroscopes Made Easy:
The "RIGHT-WAY" Guide to Using Gem Identification Tools

2014 Paperback Edition, First Printing

The Library of Congress has cataloged the previous edition of *Gem Identification Made Easy*, from which this booklet is drawn, as follows:
Matlins, Antoinette Leonard.
Gem identification made easy : a hands-on guide to more confident buying & selling. —5th edition.
    pages cm
Written by Antoinette Matlins and A.C. Bonanno.
Includes bibliographical references and index.
ISBN 978-0-943763-90-3 (hc)
1. Precious stones—Identification. I. Bonanno, Antonio C. II. Title.
    QE392.M33 2013
    553.8028'7—dc23

Some of the material in *Gem Identification Made Easy* appeared originally as articles in *National Jeweler*.

Dichroscopes Made Easy: The "RIGHT-WAY" Guide to Using Gem Identification Tools
ISBN 978-0-9904152-1-3 (pbk)
ISBN 978-0-943763-96-5 (eBook)

Cover Design: Jenny Buono, Stefan Killen and Bridgett Taylor
Text Design: James F. Brisson
Illustrations: Kathleen Robinson

10   9   8   7   6   5   4   3   2   1

Manufactured in the United States of America
Published by GemStone Press
A Division of LongHill Partners, Inc.
Sunset Farm Offices, Rte. 4, P.O. Box 237
Woodstock, VT 05091
Tel: (802) 457-4000 Fax: (802) 457-4004
www.gemstonepress.com

WHAT IS A DICHROSCOPE?

The dichroscope is one of the most important pocket instruments. As we mentioned earlier, armed with only the loupe, Chelsea filter, and dichroscope, a competent gemologist can positively identify approximately 85% of all colored gemstones. While it takes years to develop professional-level skill, knowing how to use these three instruments will start you on your way.

Like the Chelsea filter, the dichroscope is very easy to use. It is used *only* for transparent colored stones and not for colored opaque stones, or amber and opal.

The dichroscope provides one of the easiest and fastest ways for differentiating transparent stones of the same color from one another. The jeweler who knows how to use this instrument can easily distinguish, for example, a ruby from a red garnet or a red spinel (one of the popular "new" stones seen with increasing frequency); a blue sapphire from fine tanzanite or blue spinel; an amethyst from purple glass; or an emerald from many of its imitations or look-alikes.

The dichroscope we recommend is a *calcite-type* (not a polarizing type). It is a small tubular-shaped instrument that is approximately 2 inches long and ½ inch in diameter. In most models, the tube has a small round opening at one end, and a rectangular opening on the other (in these models, look through the *round* opening). Some models have two round openings, one slightly larger. Look into the dichroscope without any stone or piece of jewelry. Just hold the instrument up to the light, and look through it. Do you see two small rectangular windows at the opposite end? If not, look through the other end. The important thing is to be sure that when you look through the opening, you are looking through the end that allows you to see a pair of rectangular windows at the opposite end.

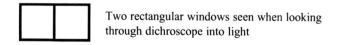
Two rectangular windows seen when looking through dichroscope into light

When colored stones are viewed with the dichroscope, some will show the same color in both rectangular windows while other stones will show two colors, or two different tones or shades of the same color. For example, you might see blue in one window and yellow in the other. Or, you might see pink in one window, and red in the other. In either case, the colors you see would be considered "two" colors, even though pink is really a lighter shade of the color red. If you were to see orangey-red in one window and violet-red in the other, this would also be considered seeing two colors, even though they are really different shades of the same color.

One can successfully use the dichroscope without understanding why only one color is seen with some stones and more than one with others. You simply need to know how to use the instrument properly, and what to look for, stone by stone. However, we think it is interesting to understand why, so we will take a moment to explain it in very simple terms.

When a ray of light enters a colored gemstone, depending on the particular properties of that stone, it will either continue travelling through as a *single* ray, or divide into *two rays*. Stones through which it continues as a single ray are said to be "single refracting"; stones through which it splits and travels as two rays are "double refracting." If you look at an object through a strongly double refracting stone such as calcite, you will actually see two images. Try it. Write your name on a piece of paper and then read it through a piece of calcite—you'll see double.

Single refracting stones are those that will always show *the same color* in both rectangular windows of the dichroscope. Only a few gemstone materials are single refracting—diamond, garnet, spinel, glass, colored YAG, colored CZ, and plastic. Therefore, if you have a stone that only exhibits one color, identity can be fairly quick, since there are so few possibilities.

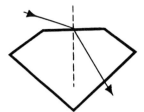 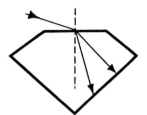

Single refraction: A ray of light enters the material and continues travelling through it as a *single* ray.

Double refraction: A ray of light enters the material and *splits* into *two rays*, each travelling at a different angle and speed.

Most gems are double refracting and will show *two colors*, one color in one rectangular window of the dichroscope, and a different color or distinctly different *shade* of color in the second window. We call these stones "dichroic" (di = two; chro = color). When a ray of light enters the stone and splits into two rays (as it does with all double-refracting stones), each of the two rays will travel through the stone *at a different angle and speed*. The angle and speed at which light travels determine the color we see. So, if we could separate the rays and see each one individually, we would see a different color for each. This is what the dichroscope does. It separates each of the two rays so we can see both colors.

Some stones show *three colors* when viewed with the dichroscope. We call these stones *trichroic* (tri = three; chro = color). These stones are also double refracting, but when light enters from certain directions we get one pair of rays (travelling at certain angles and speeds), and when it enters from another direction, we get a *different* pair. In the second pair, one of the two rays will travel at an angle and speed different from either of the two rays in the first pair. Thus the third color. We get two colors (one in each rectangular

Same color seen in both rectangular boxes of dichroscope in single-refracting stones.

Different colors, or shades of same color, seen with dichroscope in double-refracting stones.

window) in certain directions, and two colors from another direction, but not the same two colors. One of the colors in the second pair will be different from the colors seen in the first pair.

The specific color or shades of color seen through the dichroscope present a very important clue to the identity of a stone. Let's take two red stones that are approximately the same color red—ruby and red spinel—and view them through the dichroscope. We would be able to identify the ruby immediately because two distinctly different shades of color would appear, one in each of the two small rectangular windows: a strong orange-red would show up in one, and a strong purple-red in the other. However, the red spinel would exhibit the same color in both windows—there would be no difference in tone or shade of red, but exactly the same red. (*Note:* the dichroscope can separate stones that look like one another in color—ruby from glass, sapphire from spinel, and so on—but cannot separate *natural* from *synthetic*. Additional tests are required for that.)

The particular colors observed may also help you determine whether or not the color of the gem is *natural*. Such is the case with the popular, strongly trichroic blue gem called "tanzanite," a member of the zoisite family. Zoisite occurs naturally in a wide range of colors from brownish or greenish-yellow to lavender, to violet-blue or deep sapphire-blue. The lovely blue colors that are so desirable, however, are rare; most blue tanzanite is *brownish* zoisite that has been *heated*. When heated, the brownish color changes to a much prettier blue color. But heating changes more than just the body color seen; it changes the trichroic colors seen with the dichroscope. Natural color blue tanzanite exhibits three distinct, *different* colors: a pronounced blue, purple, and green are typically seen. Sometimes the purple color is very reddish, and sometimes yellow is present rather than green, but the important thing to note is that you will observe three *different* colors. "Heated" blue tanzanite, however, usually exhibits two colors—purple and blue—but you will see two different *shades* of blue, one distinctly lighter than the other, so it is still considered a "trichroic" gem. What is important to note is that the green/yellow color is usually absent in heated blue tanzanite. **When checking tanzanite with the dichroscope, the presence of green or yellow in the trichroic colors seen may indicate that the stone's blue** color is *natural*; the absence of green or yellow usually indicates *heat-induced* color.

HOW TO USE THE DICHROSCOPE

Although the dichroscope is simple to use, it is important to make sure you have proper light and that you rotate the dichroscope as we will describe below. You must also remember to view the stone from five different directions. Keeping these points in mind, proceed as follows.

1. Hold the dichroscope between your thumb and forefinger, gently resting it against the stone being examined.

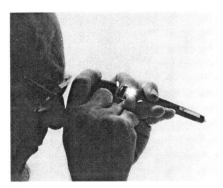

Using the dichroscope. Notice that the dichroscope is held very close to the stone and the eye. Holding the tube between the thumb and the forefinger allows easy rotation of the dichroscope as you view the stone. The light is being *transmitted* through the stone.

2. Place the eye as close as possible to the end of the dichroscope. Be sure you are looking through the end that allows you to see a pair of rectangular windows at the opposite end.
3. View the stone with strong light that is *transmitted through the stone*. A small high-intensity utility lamp is a good source for transmitted light (these lamps offer the added benefit of stronger light since the stone can be held close to the light source). A strong penlight also provides good light to use with the dichroscope. Or, use light coming from a ceiling fixture (hold the stone and dichroscope up, looking into the light, with the light coming through the back of the stone).
4. To view the stone with the dichroscope, hold the dichroscope as close as possible to the stone, even touching it (be sure a strong light is coming through the stone, from behind it).

5. Look into the dichroscope. While looking through it, slowly rotate the *dichroscope* (not the stone) at least 180 degrees. Does a second color appear in either of the windows as you rotate it? For example, while looking at ruby you may see the same color in both windows as you begin, possibly an orange-red color. Then, as you turn the dichroscope, you will see a second color appear. You will still see the orange-red color you've seen all along in one window, but in the second window the color may change to violet-red. If there is no apparent change of color in one of the windows, continue rotating the dichroscope until you have turned it a full 360 degrees. If you still don't see a second color, change the direction through which you are viewing the stone.

6. Following exactly the same procedure described above, examine the stone from another direction. You must examine the stone from *five* different directions to be sure that there is, or is not, a second (and sometimes a third) color. The five directions are: top to bottom; side to side; front to back; on a diagonal to one of those directions; on a diagonal to the other direction.

Using the ruby again as an example, if we viewed it from only one direction, even though we rotate the dichroscope, we might only see a single color in the two boxes. If we stopped here, we could draw

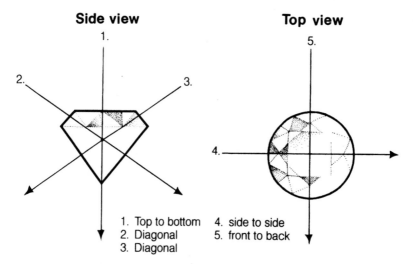

Side view   **Top view**

1. Top to bottom 4. side to side
2. Diagonal   5. front to back
3. Diagonal

Examine the stone from five directions: top-to-bottom, side-to-side, front-to-back, and from two different diagonals.

a false conclusion that a genuine ruby were a garnet or spinel. If we do not detect more than one color in the first direction, we must repeat the examination from a second direction, and again from a third direction, and so on, until we have examined it from all five directions.

REMEMBER: *AS YOU VIEW THE STONE IN EACH DIRECTION, YOU MUST ROTATE THE DICHROSCOPE.*

7. Note the color seen in each window, in each direction. You may see only one color; or two colors (in which case you are observing *dichroism*); or, in some stones, three colors *(trichroism).*

In the case of trichroic stones, you will see one pair of colors in the rectangular windows when viewed from one direction, and a second pair when viewed from a different direction. One color will be the same in both pairs.

Andalusite provides a good example of trichroism. When it is viewed with the dichroscope in one direction, you may see yellow in one window and green in the other. Then, when viewing it from another direction, you might see the same yellow you saw in the first pair of colors and, in addition, a reddish-brown in the other window.

The specific colors seen in the rectangular windows, as well as the number of colors seen (two or three), can help you make a positive identification of most colored stones. But remember, you must observe the stone from at least five different directions. A second color will often fail to show up when viewed from only one direction. And, of course, a third color, which would indicate a trichroic stone, might be present. If you think a stone might be one that exhibits trichroism, you must not stop after seeing a second color, but continue through all five directions until you have, or have not, detected the third. This can be especially important in gem identification since far fewer stones are trichroic and, therefore, the test would give positive ID on the spot.

While the dichroscope is an easy instrument to master, we recommend having someone who is already familiar with it assist you the first time. This will help insure that you are holding it properly and have the proper lighting. It shouldn't take more than 15 minutes to get the hang of it.

WHAT THE DICHROSCOPE WILL SHOW

Once you feel comfortable handling the dichroscope, you are ready to start viewing stones. If only one color is observed with the dichroscope, it usually indicates that you have a "non-dichroic" material. You can see from the following list that there are only a few gemstones in this category. If you see two colors, you have a "dichroic" (di = two; chro = color) material; if you pick up a third color, a "trichroic" (tri = three; chro = color) material.

In the following pages we have provided lists showing, both by color and by gemstone family, the colors you should see when looking at the popular gemstones with the dichroscope. Such tables are also provided in standard gemology textbooks (see "Tables on Pleochroism").

Once you note the colors you see with the dichroscope, check the chart to see which stone(s) would show those colors. If there is only one, you can now make a positive identification. If there is more than one, you may need to use the Chelsea filter, loupe or other instrument.

REMEMBER: The dichroscope can separate stones that look like one another in color—ruby from glass, sapphire from spinel, and so on—but cannot separate *natural* from *synthetic*. Additional tests are required for that.

LEARN TO USE THE THREE POCKET INSTRUMENTS TOGETHER

Sometimes a gemstone that should show dichroism doesn't. Two stones that demonstrate how checking for dichroism alone may be inconclusive for gem ID are peridot and green zircon. These exceptions offer excellent examples of how useful the loupe, Chelsea filter, and dichroscope can be in assuring accurate gem ID *when used together*.

Peridot and green zircon can resemble each other. There is also green glass that can look like both of them. The dichroic colors of green zircon will differentiate it from peridot and glass (and vice versa) when you can detect them, but sometimes they are too weak to detect. And sometimes green zircon just doesn't exhibit dichroism.

Here's where using another one of our three pocket instruments can be useful.

If you examine a green zircon with a Chelsea filter you will see a reddish coloration, which you will not see with peridot (peridot remains green when viewed with the filter). However, it could still be green glass.

Now your loupe will come to the rescue. First, the loupe may reveal "doubling." This is an optical effect that makes you think you are "seeing double." To observe doubling, look through the stone (check from several different directions). If the edges of the back facets appear double, as if you have double vision, you are seeing "doubling" (sometimes the facet edge, instead of looking like a single line, will resemble a narrow set of railroad tracks).

Zircon will exhibit doubling (peridot will also show doubling of the back facets, but we eliminated it with the Chelsea filter—since it showed reddish, it can't be peridot. Peridot would have remained green). Glass is still a possibility. However, glass will not show any doubling. Zircon does. So, by checking with the loupe to see if we can observe doubling, we can determine the identity of the stone. If we see doubling, we now know we have zircon.

If you are not sure whether or not you see doubling, the loupe will still aid you. It will tell you from the presence and type of inclusions whether it is glass or zircon. Now we will know for sure that we have zircon.

Next let's take a look at peridot. If you are able to detect trichroism, you will have no question as to the stone's identity being peridot. But peridot often shows only two colors and might be confused with green zircon. To further complicate matters, there are three types of zircon, all of which may occur in some shade of green: "low" (also called "metamict"), "intermediate," and "high." The crystalline structure of zircon has been broken down as a result of naturally occurring exposure to radiation and may exhibit virtually no double refraction, no dichroism, and no doubling; intermediate zircon has had a less severe breakdown of the crystal structure than the "low" type so it *will* exhibit double-refraction, weak dichroism, and doubling (but less strong than peridot); "high" zircon has strong double refraction, and will exhibit good dichroism and very strong doubling, even greater than peridot. *Usually* green zircon is either "low" or "intermediate" so seeing strong doubling would lead us to conclude the stone is peridot. Furthermore, "high" zircon is also typically light green, while peridot can be medium to deep green. So if the color is a deeper green, strong doubling might lead us to conclude the stone is peridot. Peridot is also encountered far more frequently than green zircon. Nonetheless, in this example, you might not be able to make a positive determination with just the loupe and dichroscope. Here again, using another instrument, in this case the Chelsea filter, will give you the answer. If the stone is peridot, it will remain greenish when viewed through the filter, but if it is green zircon it will look *reddish* through the filter.

Another important use of the dichroscope is for separating tanzanite from its imitations. Many imitations are single-refracting and exhibit no dichroism, while tanzanite is trichroic. Synthetic corundum (sapphire) is produced in tanzanite colors, but it is dichroic and produces different dichroic colors from tanzanite. Synthetic forsterite could be mistaken for tanzanite, but it is also dichroic, not trichroic. However, one of the colors seen in forsterite (purplish pink) might suggest tanzanite, especially if mounted in a way to prevent checking from multiple directions. In such cases, examination with an ultraviolet lamp or refractometer will instantly indicate whether or not it is tanzanite.

Practice using these three pocket instruments together. Within a surprisingly short period of time, you'll become much more confident, and begin to enjoy the rewards of accurate gem ID.

COLORS EXHIBITED BY POPULAR DICHROIC AND TRICHROIC GEMS—BY GEM COLOR

2-Dichroic 3-Trichroic	S-Strong D-Distinct W-Weak
Note: Light-colored stones exhibit weak dichroism—hard to detect	

Gemstone	Dichroic or Trichroic	Intensity of Color	Colors Seen
PURPLE OR VIOLET GEMS			
CHRYSOBERYL			
Alexandrite	3	S in deep colors	In natural light: emerald-green/ yellowish/reddish In artificial light: emerald-green/ reddish-yellow/red
Synthetic Alexandrite (corundum-type)	2	S in deep colors	In natural light: brownish-green/ mauve In artificial light: brownish-yellow/mauve
CORUNDUM			
Violet Sapphire	2	S	yellowish-red/violet; or pale gray/ green
QUARTZ			
Amethyst	2	D to W	purple/reddish-purple; or purple/ blue
SPODUMENE			
Kunzite (lavender)	3	S	colorless/pink/violet
TOURMALINE			
Purple/Violet	2	S	purple/light purple
ZOISITE			
Tanzanite	3	S	blue/purplish or reddish/green or yellow; or blue/lighter blue/purplish or reddish [Note: the presence of *green* or *yellow* may indicate *natural* color.]
BLUE GEMS			
BENITOITE	2	S	colorless/indigo-blue (or greenish-blue)
BERYL			
Aquamarine	2	S to W	Blue variety: blue/colorless Blue-green variety: pale blue-green/pale yellow-green to colorless
CORUNDUM			
Blue Sapphire	2	S	greenish-blue/deep blue

12

Gem			
FORSTERITE			
(Synthetic)	2	S	blue/purplish pink
IOLITE			
(Dichroite)	3	S	pale blue/pale straw-yellow/ dark violet-blue
TOPAZ			
Blue	3	S to D	colorless/pale blue/pale pink (Note: pink usually is imperceptible.)
TOURMALINE			
Indicolite (blue)	2	S	light blue/dark blue
Blue-Green	2	S	light blue-green/dark blue-green
ZIRCON			
Blue	2	D	colorless/blue
ZOISITE			
(Tanzanite)	3	S	blue/purplish or reddish/green or yellow; or blue/lighter blue/purplish or reddish [Note: the presence of *green* or *yellow* may indicate *natural* color.]

GREEN GEMS

Gem			
ANDALUSITE (green)	3	S	brownish-green/olive-green/ flesh-red
BERYL			
Emerald	2	S to W	yellowish-green/bluish-green
CHRYSOBERYL			
Alexandrite	3	S in deep colors	In natural light: emerald green/ yellowish/reddish In artificial light: emerald-green/ reddish-yellow/red
Synthetic Alexandrite (Corundum-type)	2	S in deep colors	In natural light: brownish-green/ mauve In artificial light: brownish-yellow/mauve
CORUNDUM			
Green Sapphire	2	S	yellowish-green/green
PERIDOT	3	D to W	yellow-green/green/yellowish [Note: It often is difficult to detect two colors; the third usually is imperceptible.]
SPODUMENE			
Hiddenite (green)	3	S	bluish-green/grass-green/ yellowish-green or colorless
TOURMALINE			
Green	2	S	pale green/ strong green; or brownish-green/dark green [Note: If you see *red* through Chelsea filter, it's Chrome Tourmaline.]

| ZIRCON | 2 | W | brownish-green/green (or colorless) |

YELLOW GEMS

Gem			
BERYL			
Heliodor (yellow)	2	S to W	pale yellow-green/ pale bluish-green
CHRYSOBERYL			
Yellow	3	S in deep colors	colorless/pale yellow/ lemon-yellow
CORUNDUM			
Yellow sapphire	2	D to W	very weak yellowish tints
QUARTZ			
Citrine	2	D to W	yellow/paler yellow (or colorless)
SPODUMENE			
Yellow	3	S	yellow/pale yellow/deep yellow
TOPAZ			
Yellow	3	S to D	honey-yellow/straw-yellow/ pinkish-yellow [Note: In topaz, a third color seldom is seen.]
TOURMALINE			
Yellow	2	S	light yellow/dark yellow
ZIRCON			
Yellow	2	W	brownish-yellow/yellow

BROWN OR ORANGE GEMS

Gem			
CORUNDUM Sapphire	2	S	yellowish-brown to orange/ colorless
QUARTZ Smoky	2	D to W	brownish/reddish-brown [clear differentiation]
TOPAZ Brown/Orange	3	D	colorless/yellow-brown/brown
TOURMALINE Brown/Orange	2	S	yellow-brown/deep brown; or brownish-green/dark green
ZIRCON Brown	2	W	yellow-brown/reddish brown

RED/PINK GEMS

Gem			
BERYL			
Morganite (pink)	2	S to W	pale rose/bluish rose
Red (red "emerald")	2	S	orange-red/purple-red
CHRYSOBERYL			
Alexandrite	3	S in deep colors	In natural light: emerald-green/yellowish/reddish In artificial light: emerald-green/ reddish-yellow/red
Synthetic Alexandrite (Corundum-type)	2	S in deep colors	In natural light: brownish-green/ mauve In artificial light: brownish-yellow/mauve

CORUNDUM			
Ruby	2	S	orangish-red/purple-red
Pink Sapphire	2	S to W	Two slightly different shades of pink; often difficult, if not impossible, to detect in pale stones.
DIASPORE (color-change "Zultanite")	3	S	bluish, greenish, yellowish (easiest to see third color when viewed in diffused, full-spectrum daylight such as found outdoors on a sunny day, away from direct sunlight)
QUARTZ Rose	2	D to W	pink/pale pink [clear differentiation]
TOPAZ Pink	2	S to W	colorless/very pale pink/pink
TOURMALINE Rubellite (Red)	2	S	pink/dark red (or magenta)
ZIRCON Red	2	W	clove-brown/reddish-brown

Popular Gems' Usual Dichroic or Trichroic Colors by Gem Family

2-Dichroic 3-Trichroic		S-Strong D-Distinct W-Weak	
Note: Light-colored stones exhibit weak dichroism—hard to detect			
Gemstone	Dichroic or Trichroic	Intensity of Color	Colors Seen
ANDALUSITE (green)	3	S	brownish-green/olive-green/ flesh-red
BENITOITE	2	S	colorless/indigo-blue (or greenish-blue)
BERYL			
Emerald	2	S to W	yellowish-green/bluish-green
Aquamarine	2	S to W	Blue variety: blue/colorless Blue-green variety: pale blue-green/pale yellow-green (or colorless)
Morganite (pink)	2	S to W	pale rose/bluish-rose
Red ("red emerald")	2	S	orange-red/purple-red
Heliodor (yellow)	2	S to W	pale yellow-green/ pale bluish-green

CHRYSOBERYL			
Yellow	3	S in deep colors	colorless/pale yellow/ lemon-yellow
Alexandrite	3	S in deep colors	In natural light: emerald-green/ yellowish/reddish In artificial light: emerald-green/ reddish-yellow/red
Synthetic Alexandrite (Corundum-type)	2	S in deep colors	In natural light: brownish-green/ mauve In artificial light: brownish-yellow/mauve
CORUNDUM			
Ruby	2	S	orangish-red/purple-red
Blue Sapphire	2	S	greenish-blue/deep-blue
Green Sapphire	2	S	yellowish-green/green
Orange/Brown Sapphire	2	S	yellowish-brown to orange/colorless
Pink Sapphire	2	S	two slightly different shades of pink; often difficult, if not impossible, to detect in pale stones
Violet Sapphire	2	S	yellowish-red/violet; or pale gray/green
Yellow Sapphire	2	D to W	very weak yellowish tints
DIASPORE (color-change "Zultanite")	3	S	bluish, greenish, yellowish
IOLITE (Dichroite)	3	S	pale blue/pale straw-yellow/ dark violet-blue
PERIDOT	3	D to W	yellow-green/green/yellowish [Note: it often is difficult to detect two colors; the third usually is imperceptible.]
QUARTZ			
Amethyst	2	D to W	purple/reddish-purple; or purple/blue
Citrine	2	D to W	yellow/paler yellow (or colorless)
Rose	2	D to W	pink/pale pink [clear differentiation]
Smoky	2	D to W	brownish/reddish-brown [clear differentiation]
SPODUMENE			
Kunzite (lavender)	3	S	colorless/pink/violet
Hiddenite (green)	3	S	bluish-green/grass-green/ yellowish-green (or colorless)
Yellow	3	S	yellow/pale yellow/deep yellow

TOPAZ			
Blue	3	S to D	colorless/pale blue/pale pink [Note: pink usually is imperceptible]
Brown/Orange	3	D	colorless/yellow-brown/brown
Pink	3	S to D	colorless/very pale pink/pink
Yellow	3	S to D	honey-yellow/straw-yellow/ pinkish-yellow [Note: in topaz, a third color seldom is seen.]
TOURMALINE			
Blue-Green	2	S	light blue-green/dark blue-green
Brown/Orange	2	S	yellow-brown/deep brown (or brown-black or greenish-brown)
Green	2	S	pale green/strong green; or brownish-green/dark green [Note: If *red* through Chelsea filter, it's Chrome Tourmaline.]
Indicolite (blue)	2	S	light blue/dark blue
Purple/Violet	2	S	purple/light purple
Rubellite (red)	2	S	pink/dark red (or magenta)
ZIRCON			
Blue	2	D	colorless/blue
Brown	2	W	yellow-brown/reddish-brown
Green	2	W	brownish-green/green (or colorless)
Red	2	W	clove-brown/reddish-brown
Yellow	2	W	brownish-yellow/yellow
ZOISITE (Tanzanite)	3	S	blue/purplish or reddish/green or yellow; or blue/lighter blue/purplish or reddish [Note: the presence of *green* or *yellow* usually indicates *natural* color.]

"Gems" That Show No Dichroism

Garnet
Spinel & Synthetic Spinel
Colored Diamond
Colored Diamond Simulants (CZ, YAG, etc.)
Glass
Plastic

About the "RIGHT-WAY" Series on Using Gem Identification Tools

The Antoinette Matlins "RIGHT-WAY" Series is a set of essential booklets that explains in non-technical terms how to use individual gem identification instruments to identify diamonds and colored gems, and how to separate natural gems from imitations, treated gemstones, synthetics, and look-alikes. The approach is direct and practical, and its style is easy to understand. In fact, with these highly accessible guide booklets, anyone can begin to master gem identification. The booklet series is based on the bestselling book *Gem Identification Made Easy: A Hands-On Guide to More Confident Buying & Selling* (5th Edition) by Antoinette Matlins, PG, FGA, and A. C. Bonanno, FGA, ASA, MGA.

Using a simple, step-by-step system developed by the authors, the series explains how to properly use essential but uncomplicated instruments to identify gems by explaining what to look for gemstone by gemstone. The key to avoiding costly mistakes and recognizing profitable opportunities is knowing both what to look for and what to look out for. In total, it is a basic introduction to gem identification that will enable anyone interested in gems to understand how to identify them.

THE CONCEPTS

Each booklet in the series explores one or more gem identification instruments, and provides an overview of when and why to use them, step-by-step instructions on how to use each, and what will be shown—or not be shown. It guides the reader on using each instrument with any precious gemstones they are trying to identify.

Chelsea and Synthetic
Emerald Filters Made Easy
978-0-9904152-0-6

Dichroscopes Made Easy
978-0-9904152-1-3

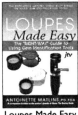

Loupes Made Easy
978-0-9904152-2-0

Refractometers Made Easy
978-0-9904152-0-6

SSEF Diamond-Type Spotter and
Blue Diamond Tester Made Easy
978-0-9904152-5-1

Ultraviolet Lamps
Made Easy
978-0-9904152-4-4

Antoinette Matlins, PG, FGA, is an internationally respected gem and jewelry expert, author and lecturer. Honored with the international Accredited Gemologists Association's highest award for excellence in gemology, Ms. Matlins's books are published in seven languages and are widely used throughout the world by consumers and professionals in the gem and jewelry field. Her books include *Gem Identification Made Easy: A Hands-On Guide to More Confident Buying & Selling; Jewelry & Gems: The Buying Guide* (over 400,000 copies now in print—the only book of its kind ever offered by *Consumer Reports*); and *Jewelry & Gems at Auction: The Definitive Guide to Buying & Selling at the Auction House & on Internet Auction Sites* (all from GemStone Press).

Former gemology editor of *National Jeweler* magazine, her articles and comments on buying and selling gems and jewelry and on gem investment have appeared in many national and international consumer and trade publications. She is also the author of the "Gemstones" chapter in the *Encyclopedia of Investments,* 2nd Edition.

Ms. Matlins has gained wide recognition as a dedicated consumer advocate. She has spearheaded the Accredited Gemologists Association's nationwide campaign against gemstone investment telemarketing scams. A popular media guest, she has been seen on ABC, CBS, NBC and CNN educating consumers about gems and jewelry and exposing fraud.

In addition to her educational work, Ms. Matlins is retained by clients worldwide to seek fine, rare or unusual gems and jewels for acquisition.

For more information on seminars and workshops given by Antoinette Matlins, visit www.gemstonepress.com.

OTHER BOOKS BY ANTOINETTE MATLINS

Colored Gemstones: The Antoinette Matlins Buying Guide

Diamonds: The Antoinette Matlins Buying Guide

Engagement & Wedding Rings: The Definitive Buying Guide for People in Love

*Gem Identification Made Easy: A Hands-On Guide
to More Confident Buying & Selling*

*Jewelry & Gems at Auction: The Definitive Guide to Buying & Selling
at the Auction House & on Internet Auction Sites*

Jewelry & Gems: The Buying Guide

The Pearl Book: The Definitive Buying Guide

GemStone Press
Helping to increase understanding, appreciation and enjoyment of jewelry, gems and gemology.

GemStone Press is an international source for books, gem-identification equipment and other items designed to help consumers and people in the gem trade learn more about jewelry, gems and gemology.

GemStone Press books are easy to read, easy to use. They are designed for the person who does not have a scientific or technical background.

Visit www.gemstonepress.com/category/GII.html for more information on our extensive selection of gem identification equipment. All gem identification equipment we supply has been tested and chosen by Antoinette Matlins for its quality.

GemStone Press
Sunset Farm Offices, Route 4
P.O. Box 237 • Woodstock, VT 05091
Tel (802) 457-4000   Fax (802) 457-4004
Orders: (800) 962-4544 (8:30AM–5:30PM ET Mon.–Fri.)
www.gemstonepress.com

CPSIA information can be obtained at www.ICGtesting.com
Printed in the USA
BVOW05s1451310714

360452BV00011B/76/P